Dangerous Creatures

of the
Oceans

Helen Bateman and Jayne Denshire

Smart Apple Media

This edition first published in 2005 in the United States of America by Smart Apple Media.

Smart Apple Media
1980 Lookout Drive
North Mankato
Minnesota 56003

First published in 2005 by
MACMILLAN EDUCATION AUSTRALIA PTY LTD
627 Chapel Street, South Yarra 3141

Visit our website at www.macmillan.com.au

Associated companies and representatives throughout the world.

Copyright © Helen Bateman and Jayne Denshire 2005

Library of Congress Cataloging-in-Publication Data

Bateman, Helen.
   Of the oceans / by Helen Bateman and Jayne Denshire.
   p. cm. – (Dangerous creatures)
   Includes index.

   ISBN 1-58340-768-5

   1. Dangerous marine animals—Juvenile literature. I. Denshire, Jayne. II. Title.
   QL122.2B38 2005
   691.77—dc22

                                                     2005042866

Project management by Limelight Press Pty Ltd
Design by Stan Lamond, Lamond Art & Design
Illustrations by Edwina Riddell
Maps by Laurie Whiddon, Map Illustrations. Adapted by Lamond Art & Design
Research by Kate McAllan

Consultant: George McKay PhD, Conservation Biologist

Printed in China

Acknowledgments
The authors and the publisher are grateful to the following for permission to reproduce copyright material:

Cover photograph: orca beaching to catch a South American sea lion, courtesy of D. Parer & E. Parer-Cook/AUSCAPE.

Ben Cropp/AUSCAPE pp. 9, 10; Tui De Roy/AUSCAPE p. 26; Jeff Foott/AUSCAPE p. 20; APL/Corbis/Anthony Bannister p. 18; APL/John & Lorraine Carnemolla p. 11; APL/Corbis/Patricia Fogden p. 19; APL/Corbis/Stephen Frink p. 23; APL/Corbis/Chris Hellier p. 16; APL/Corbis/Kevin Schafer p. 6; Corbis pp. 7, 27; Clay Bryce/Lochman Transparencies pp. 13 (bottom), 14, 15, 17, 25, 28; Peter & Margy Nicholas/Lochman Transparencies pp. 13 (top), 22, 29; Nature Scenes PhotoDisc p. 5; PhotoDisc pp. 12, 21; David Fleetham/Photolibrary.com p. 8.

Please note
At the time of printing, the Internet addresses appearing in this book were correct. Owing to the dynamic nature of the Internet, however, we cannot guarantee that all these addresses will remain correct.

Contents

When a word is printed in **bold**, you can look up its meaning in the Glossary on page 31.

Life in the oceans

More than two-thirds of the Earth's surface is covered by seas and oceans, which are home to thousands of types of animals. Different creatures live in different areas of the ocean. Some live in the shallow water near coastlines. Others live in the deeper water of the open ocean. Still more live in the depths of the ocean or even on the ocean floor.

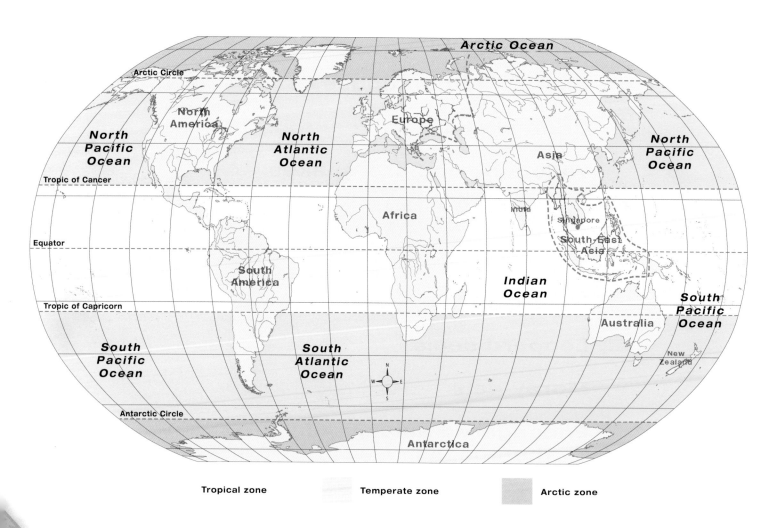

Tropical zone   Temperate zone   Arctic zone

▲ The oceans of the world are classified into
three main zones depending on how far they are
from the equator. These are called the tropical
zone, temperate zone, and the arctic zone.

▲ The ocean is
home to many
thousands of
creatures. Most
of them are not
dangerous to
humans.

Danger and survival

Animals living in the oceans behave dangerously because they need
to survive in their **habitat**. All creatures have to find food and
shelter and often need to defend themselves against other animals at
the same time. For many creatures, it is a case of kill or be killed.

Some ocean creatures live on plants, but most
have to hunt and eat other animals to
survive. Some creatures are dangerous
to humans, but usually only if
they feel threatened by them.

The top **predators** of the
oceans are killer whales.
They are the highest level of the
oceans' natural **food chain**. They
eat sharks and large fish that
make up the level below. These
in turn eat smaller fish from the
third level of the chain. Smaller
fish eat prawns and other tiny
creatures that feed on sea
plants, the lowest level
of the chain.

killer whale

shark

sea plant

prawns

fish

▲ The ocean food chain has five links or
levels. The animals from each level survive
by eating something from the level below.

Killer whales

Killer whales, or orcas, are the largest of all the dolphins. They are found in almost every ocean in the world. They have a large **dorsal fin** and distinctive markings. Their back is shiny black with a patch of light grey, and their stomach is white. They have a large white area above each eye. Killer whales are dangerous to more than 200 types of animal, but not to humans. They hunt other whales, seals, fish, squid, sharks, turtles, sea otters, walrus, and birds such as penguins and gulls.

▲ Killer whales, or orcas, are also called "wolves of the sea" because they hunt in packs just like wolves do on land.

Community living

Killer whales live together in communities called **pods**. They take good care of their young and protect them from danger. The older whales teach the younger ones how to hunt.

Group hunting

Killer whales are really successful hunters because of the way they cooperate with each other, working in groups to catch their **prey**.

Often when killer whales are hunting fish, they herd them into a group so that they are easier to attack. When they are hunting penguins or seals, sometimes one whale bumps them off the ice, or scares them into jumping into the water where the other whales are waiting. Some killer whales even splash the water with their tail to make waves that will wash the prey off the ice into the water.

▲ Killer whales often poke their head straight up out of the water to see if there is anything nearby that they can eat.

fact flash

Killer whales do not chew their food. They swallow seals and sea lions whole. Their teeth are used for biting and tearing, not chewing.

sound from whale

echo returning to whale

▲ Killer whales find their prey by making clicking sounds and listening for their echoes. They can tell how close their prey is by how quickly the echo returns to them. The faster the echo, the closer the prey.

Tiger sharks

VITAL STATISTICS

LENGTH
up to 24 feet (7.4 m)

WEIGHT
up to one ton (1 t)

WHERE FOUND
tropical and warm temperate waters

Tiger sharks are large and dangerous. Their barrel-shaped body is blue-gray to brown on the top, and yellow to light gray or even white underneath. When they are young they have black or dark gray stripes on their back. These markings, which give them their name, fade as they grow older.

DANGER REPORT

On October 31, 2003, an up-and-coming 13-year-old surfer was savagely attacked by a tiger shark in the waters of Kaua'i, Hawaii.

The shark bit off her left arm, just below the shoulder. A family friend helped her to shore, saving her life. The young girl recovered and has since returned to surfing.

Tiger sharks are found in waters all around the world. They often swim close to shore near beaches and in bays to feed, especially at night. This makes them dangerous to humans as well as to their natural prey. Tiger sharks are said to have killed more people than great white sharks have. They are quite slow swimmers, but they can suddenly move very quickly when they are hunting.

▲ Tiger sharks are built for bursts of speed. Their body is long and streamlined, so that it is thicker at the head and thinner near the tail.

fact flash

Tiger sharks can even catch young birds that are close to the shoreline if they not strong fliers or swimmers.

► A tiger shark grows new teeth throughout its life. These teeth replace old and broken ones.

Size and strength

Tiger sharks have a large, wide mouth, a very strong jaw, and sharp, jagged teeth that can bite through a turtle's shell. Tiger sharks hunt a wide range of prey, including dolphins, large fish, sea birds, stingrays, turtles, poisonous jellyfish, and octopuses. They also **scavenge** from dead creatures such as whales.

Tiger sharks will swallow almost anything they find in the water. Items such as car licence plates, paint cans, and shoes have been found in tiger sharks' stomachs.

Cautious hunters

Tiger sharks can be careful, determined hunters, sometimes following their prey for some time. They often **stalk** their prey, staying well back from it and circling while they decide whether or not to attack. Sometimes they even take a small sample bite before they make their final strike.

fact flash

Tiger sharks swallow their prey whole or in large chunks. Later, they vomit up large bones and other objects.

Box jellyfish

Box jellyfish (also called sea wasps) are the most dangerous **stingers** in the ocean world. Their body, or bell, is often as large as a soccer ball. Up to 60 long **tentacles** hang from each of the bell's four corners. They prefer to swim in cloudy inshore waters and beaches rather than in the clear waters of a reef. Unfortunately, this is where people also like to swim. Box jellyfish are not deliberately dangerous to humans, but they will sting people if they bump into them.

▲ Box jellyfish use a form of jet propulsion, forcing a jet of water out of their body to make them move quite quickly in the opposite direction.

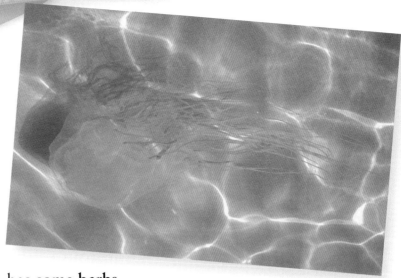

Poisonous stings

Each tentacle of a box jellyfish is covered with thousands of stinging cells that fire tiny poisonous **harpoons** into the body of the prey. Each harpoon has some **barbs** on the end. How dangerous the sting is depends on how much of the tentacle comes in contact with the victim. If an adult human touches about ten feet (3 m) of tentacle, that is enough to kill. In Australia, more than 70 people have died from box jellyfish stings in the last 100 years. This is more than the number killed by sharks and crocodiles combined.

▲ Box jellyfish are almost see-through, which makes them difficult to see when they are against a light background such as sand.

Netting prey

Sometimes box jellyfish wait for prey to bump into their tentacles, and sometimes they go after it. They gather it up with their tentacles, killing it with their **venom**. Then they pull the animal up to the bell, where they eat it. Smaller box jellyfish eat mainly prawns while the larger ones eat mainly fish.

fact flash

Turtles eat box jellyfish. They are not affected by their sting.

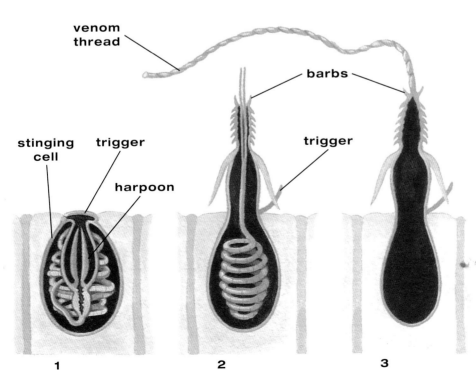

venom thread

barbs

stinging cell

trigger

trigger

harpoon

1

2

3

◄ 1 A harpoon inside each stinging cell is covered by a trigger.
2 The harpoon is fired when the trigger is brushed by the prey.
3 The barbs on the end of the harpoon attach to the victim and the thread carries the venom.

Sea anemones

VITAL STATISTICS

WIDTH
from a few inches to
three feet (1 m) across
the top

WHERE FOUND
worldwide

Sea anemones may look like harmless flowers, but they are actually **carnivorous** predators capable of catching and eating a number of small sea animals. They spend their lives attached to a hard surface, such as a rock or more commonly, the sea bottom, although they can slide around very slowly. They live in all the oceans of the world in coastal and shallow waters, and in deep trenches.

Protection

The tentacles of the sea anemone protect it from predators and help it to catch its food. Anemones that live in a **tidal zone** can draw their tentacles in when the tide goes down and then inflate them to make them rise again as the tide comes up. This keeps the tentacles safe, and prevents them from drying out.

◄ People who touch anemones do not always get stung. Sometimes the stinging cells just feel sticky.

Catching a meal

Sea anemones eat fish, prawns, small crabs, and worms. Their sticky tentacles attach themselves to the prey, inject it with the poison from their poisonous cells, and pull it into their mouth to be eaten.

fact flash

Butterflyfish eat sea anemones. They wait until the clownfish are gone and then strike.

▲ Anemones let clownfish live and hide in them. In return, the clownfish clean the anemone's tentacles. Clownfish are immune to a sea anemone's sting.

◄ The sea anemone's tentacles are covered with thousands of stinging cells. These inject venom into the prey by means of barbs that are like harpoons.

13

Blue-ringed octopuses

VITAL STATISTICS

LENGTH
tentacle up to
four inches (10 cm)

WEIGHT
up to seven ounces
(200 g)

WHERE FOUND
Australia, Singapore,
India, Southeast Asia,
and New Zealand

Blue-ringed octopuses are the most dangerous species of octopus in the world. They are shy animals that live in warm, shallow reefs off coastal areas. They have eight arms, each with two rows of harmless suction caps, and a strong, sharp beak, which they use to break open the shells of crabs. They are not aggressive towards humans and react only when they are provoked. Usually they hide among rocks and empty shells in the daytime, and come out at night to search for their food.

▲ Blue-ringed octopuses flash their bright blue rings when they are disturbed. They do this to scare predators away.

Danger signal

Normally, blue-ringed octopuses are a yellow-brown colour, which acts as a good **camouflage**. But when they are in danger, their rings flash a bright blue. Their powerful venom is produced by two large **salivary glands** and is squirted from their mouth. Their sting is not painful. In fact, some people are not even aware they have been bitten.

Food to go

Blue-ringed octopuses have two methods of hunting their prey, which is usually a **crustacean** or fish. If they are very hungry, they will grab a crab, pierce it with their beak and inject their venom. If they are not in a hurry, they will swim over the top of the crab and spray the venom into the water near it. When the venom has paralyzed the crab, they break open the shell to get to the meat inside.

DANGER REPORT

The first known death caused by a southern blue-ringed octopus was reported in Australia in June 1967.

A 23-year-old army soldier picked up an octopus from a rock pool near Sydney Harbour to show his friends. He felt nothing and did not realize he had been stung. After about ten minutes he became dizzy and his lips and tongue became numb. Soon he was unable to breathe, and within an hour and a half he was dead.

▼ When blue-ringed octopuses are not flashing their blue rings, their dull color makes them harder to see.

fact flash

If a blue-ringed octopus loses one of its arms, it will grow a new one.

Cone shells

VITAL STATISTICS

LENGTH
up to five inches
(13 cm)

WEIGHT
up to four pounds
(2 kg)

WHERE FOUND
coastal waters
in tropical and
temperate regions

Cone shells are one of the deadliest predators of the marine world. They are **mollusks** with beautiful shells, and it is the beauty of their shells that leads humans into danger. People want to collect cone shells for their colorful markings and patterns.

Cone shells are found in tropical and temperate waters. They rest during the day, buried in sand or under rocks in the same waters that humans use for wading and swimming. When people pick cone shells up, they will often receive a painful sting.

Slow and steady

Cone shells hunt at night. They move slowly over the ocean floor feeling about with their **proboscis**. This is the long part of their mouth that is shaped like a tube and protrudes from the narrow end of their shell. The proboscis stores poison darts that cone shells use when hunting. Some cone shells prey on marine worms. Others eat snails and other mollusks. The most poisonous cone shells attack small fish.

◀ There are at least 300 species of cone shell. Many of them are harmless, but it is very difficult to tell which cone shells are dangerous and which are harmless.

fact flash

Each time a cone shell uses a dart to kill a victim, it needs to be replaced. New darts are made and stored in a special pouch joined to the proboscis, just waiting to be used.

Firing line

When a cone shell detects prey, it pushes up hard against it and shoots it with a sharp, hollow dart that injects it with venom. The dart is fired from the tip of the cone shell's proboscis. It has a barb at its end that hooks into the victim and makes it almost impossible for the animal to get away. When the victim is paralyzed, the cone shell pulls it back into its proboscis, where it is digested.

▲ The proboscis of a cone shell pokes out of the narrow end of its shell. It can reach out and right over the cone shell's back.

Yellow-bellied sea snakes

Yellow-bellied sea snakes are the only sea snakes that live in the open ocean. They do not lay eggs, but give birth to live babies in the water. They float on the surface of the sea, often around drifting branches or weed. These snakes are shy animals that hunt only for their food. They usually swim away from people, but they will bite if people try to touch them.

Color warning

Yellow-bellied sea snakes have bright yellow and black scales, which are a warning to predators to stay away. They have short fangs, but their venom is very toxic, and fast acting. They close their nostrils when they dive underwater to get away from rough weather. These snakes can stay underwater for up to two hours.

◄ Sea snakes do not usually come in to land, not even to breed. Sometimes they are washed up onto the beach by a storm and have to wriggle their way back to the water.

18

Varied diet

Yellow-bellied sea snakes search for their prey of fish, eels, and prawns in cracks in rocks, and coral. Sometimes, when these snakes are floating near weeds, small fish hide under the snake without noticing it, especially around the snake's tail. Once several fish have gathered, the snake will suddenly attack, shooting backwards through the water and swiping sideways at the fish with its fangs.

Often, yellow-bellied sea snakes will try to catch larger prey. They will sometimes trap it against a reef, biting at it or simply scratching it with their fangs. Their venom is so powerful that a scratch is enough to kill their prey. They just wait for it to take effect and then pounce.

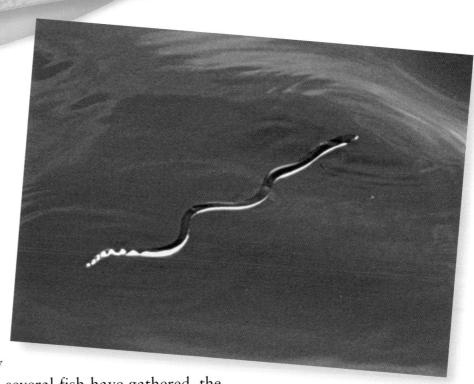

▲ Sea snakes move quickly through the water by pushing their broad tail from side to side.

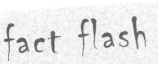

fact flash

Sea snakes usually swallow fish headfirst. This makes swallowing easier because the fish's scales do not rub the wrong way against the snake's throat.

sea snake

land snake

▶ Sea snakes have a narrow, flattened body that ends in an oar-shaped tail. Land snakes have a broad, almost circular body.

19

Sea otters

VITAL STATISTICS

LENGTH
up to five feet (1.5 m)

WEIGHT
up to 79 pounds (36 kg)

WHERE FOUND
north Pacific Ocean

Sea otters are the smallest of the marine **mammals**. They have a long body, short legs, a thick tail, and webbed back feet. They have thick fur, which they spend many hours grooming to keep it clean so it is waterproof. Sea otters are very efficient hunters and can catch enough food in three hours to last them for a whole day. They hunt a wide range of prey, but are not dangerous to humans. Sea otters hardly ever come onto land. They often even give birth to their pups at sea.

Super senses

Sea otters can see well under water, which helps them chase their prey. They have a strong sense of smell that helps them hunt at night. Their sensitive whiskers help them feel around the ocean bottom for food. They have large lungs and can stay under water for more than four minutes at a time in search of their prey.

▼ Sea otters have a flat, broad tail that is shaped like a paddle, and back feet that are shaped like flippers.

fact flash

Instead of having a layer of fat to keep them warm, sea otters have over 23,250 hairs per square inch.

A seafood feast

Sea otters eat clams, mussels, abalones, worms, crabs, and fish. They can even catch sea birds that are sitting on the surface of the water. Sea otters chase animals like crabs or fish, using their front paws to help them grab hold of their victim. They are clever hunters and sometimes use stones to scrape shellfish off rocks. They can also dive more than 131 feet (40 m) to the sea floor, where they dig for clams and worms.

▲ Sea otters use their large, strong teeth to crunch through the shells of crabs, and through bony fish heads.

Barracudas

VITAL STATISTICS

LENGTH
up to eight feet
(2.4 m)

WEIGHT
up to 176 pounds
(80 kg)

WHERE FOUND
tropical waters

Barracudas live in warm, tropical waters around reefs where they can find plenty of small fish to eat. They are large fish with a big mouth full of sharp, pointed teeth. When they are hunting, they are capable of lightning bursts of speed, and are much faster than many sharks. They are not usually aggressive to humans, but there have been some attacks reported, mostly on divers who are spreading bait or carrying speared fish.

fact flash

Once barracudas reach about 44 pounds (20 kg) they leave their school and live by themselves.

Safety in numbers

Barracudas live in schools, which makes it harder for their predators to pick out just one fish to attack. Staying together in schools also helps barracudas to hunt more successfully. As a group, they attack other schools of fish from many different directions. The smaller fish panic and forget to swim together. This makes it easier for barracudas to attack single fish.

Feeding frenzy

When barracudas prey on schools of fish, they do not always hunt just one. Sometimes they charge at the whole school, slashing at it wildly with their mouth open. Then they swim back to pick up any fish that are dead or injured. Barracudas swallow smaller fish whole. They tear off large chunks of flesh from any prey that is too large to be swallowed whole.

▲ A barracuda's sharp teeth are perfect for slashing and grabbing at prey.

◄ The markings and aggressive hunting methods of barracudas have earned them the name "tigers of the sea."

fact flash

Barracudas have attacked divers wearing bright jewelry. A flash of metal in the sun looks like sunlight reflecting off the scales of a silver fish. The barracuda sees the flash, thinks it is a fish, and attacks.

Stonefish

VITAL STATISTICS

LENGTH
up to 13 inches
(33 cm)

WHERE FOUND
Indian and Pacific
oceans

Stonefish are one of the most venomous fish in the world, but they use their venom in self-defense rather than to attack prey. They are common in reefs and shallow waters where people swim and fish. Humans are usually stung when they accidentally step on the stonefish lying on the ocean floor.

Clever cover

Stonefish are covered in lumps and bumps, and colored just like a stone. Their warty skin is covered in slime, which helps mud and **algae** to stick to it. They sit almost buried in the sand, well protected by their camouflage, and hardly ever move. They have 13 poisonous spines on their back that usually remain folded, but which are raised as a defense when the stonefish are disturbed. Stonefish do not deliberately inject venom. It is forced from the **venom sacs** out of the spine when it is squashed by the victim. The victim does all the work.

fact flash

Each stinging spine of a stonefish carries enough venom to kill a human being.

fact flash

A few weeks after a stonefish uses its venom, the skin grows back over the spine and the venom sacs refill.

▶ 1 A stonefish's spine sits under a covering of skin.
2 When a person treads on it, the covering is pushed down, away from the spine.
3 The venom is squeezed into the wound through the spine.

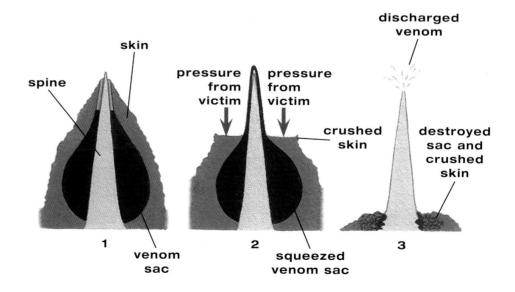

skin

spine

discharged venom

pressure from victim

pressure from victim

crushed skin

destroyed sac and crushed skin

1

venom sac

2

squeezed venom sac

3

Deaths from stonefish stings are rare. There have been five reported worldwide, but they are difficult to confirm. The sting is extremely painful. The victim feels sick, and often vomits and becomes paralyzed for a short time. Treating the sting with hot water can help, but the victim may have to go to the hospital.

Sneak attack

Stonefish are **ambush hunters**. They sit without moving on the muddy or rocky sea bottom and wait for prey, such as a small fish or crustacean, to swim past. As it does, they open their large mouth, lunge at the prey and suck it in, all with incredible speed.

▲ Stonefish are almost impossible to see. Their blotchy coloring is a perfect camouflage, blending with the ocean bottom.

25

Leopard seals

VITAL STATISTICS

LENGTH
up to 13 feet (4 m)

WEIGHT
up to 992 pounds
(450 kg)

WHERE FOUND
Antarctica

Leopard seals are one of the top predators of the Antarctic. Named for their spotted coats and huge, strong jaws, they are powerful swimmers who spend most of their life in the water. They have been known to stalk people. Scientists do not know whether this is because they are just curious about the people, or whether they are sizing them up as possible prey. Leopard seals hunt squid, other seals, krill, penguins, and other sea birds.

▲ Leopard seals have a large head with strong jaws and long, strong teeth that can easily bite through large prey.

Powerful swimmers

Although leopard seals are big and heavy, they have a streamlined body and propel themselves quickly through the water using their powerful front flippers. Leopard seals are also excellent divers. Not many animals are safe when leopard seals are hungry and on the prowl.

Food patrol

Leopard seals usually patrol the water near penguin and fur seal **colonies**. When the penguins and young seals enter the water, leopard seals attack them. The seals hold their victim in their jaws and shake them violently from side to side, hitting them on the water's surface until they are dead.

fact flash

Leopard seals break their prey into large pieces to eat, or often they swallow them whole.

DANGER REPORT

In July 2003, a 28-year-old British marine biologist snorkelling in Antarctica was attacked and dragged underwater by a leopard seal.

Leopard seals have also been known to attack inflatable boats. Antarctic researchers have had to fit special protective guards over their boats to prevent them from being punctured.

fact flash

Leopard seals spend most of their time in the water. They come out of the ocean only to rest, and to give birth to their pups.

▲ Leopard seals often swim quietly, with only the tip of their face above the water, so they can sneak up on their prey.

Moray eels

VITAL STATISTICS

LENGTH
up to 12 feet (3.7 m)

WEIGHT
up to 150 pounds
(68 kg)

WHERE FOUND
tropical waters

▼ Moray eels, particularly those that live in the tropics, have a wide variety of patterns and colors.

There are more than 150 types of moray eel. In the daytime they hide in crevices and rocks, but in the nighttime, they become fierce predators. Moray eels prey on fish, crustaceans, squid, and molluscs. They look fierce because of their large teeth and the way they leave their mouth open. Moray eels are not aggressive to humans, however, unless they are disturbed, or their **lair** is threatened. When they do bite humans, the bite is deep, often causing damage to the muscles and tendons. Bites from a moray eel are very likely to become infected. Some bites have even caused paralysis.

Hunting by smell

Moray eels do not have good eyesight. They rely on their powerful sense of smell to help them find their prey. They are large and heavy, with extremely powerful jaws and long, razor-sharp teeth. Some species of moray eel eat others, but because of their size and savage nature, moray eels have few natural ocean predators.

fact flash

Some moray eels are thought to have venomous fangs.

▼ Moray eels lurk in the day under ledges and in crevices. Most of the time, they have only their head out, ready to snap at passing prey.

Tied up in knots

Moray eels use the two large teeth on their bottom jaw to grab their prey. If the prey is small, they swallow it whole. If the prey is large, they lock their jaws onto it and then tie themselves into a knot. When they have a firm hold, they twist their body violently from their tail toward their head. The jerking movements help them to tear away large chunks of flesh from the fish.

fact flash

Moray eels' skin is thick and smooth. It does not have scales.

Endangered animals
of the
oceans

More than 5,000 animal species in the world today are endangered. They are in danger from their competitors and predators, and they are in danger from natural disasters, such as droughts, floods, and fires.

But the greatest threat to animals comes from the most dangerous animals of all—humans. As more and more people fill the Earth, there is less room for wildlife. Humans clear land to put up buildings. They farm land for crops or grazing, or they mine it to produce fuel. Precious wildlife habitats are destroyed.

Here are just some of the animals that are in danger of vanishing forever from the oceans of this planet.

ENDANGERED ANIMAL	WHERE FOUND
Atlantic cod	Atlantic Ocean
Blue-spotted stingray	Indian and Pacific oceans
Blue whale	All oceans
Bottlenose dolphin	All oceans except Arctic Ocean
Galápagos fur seal	North Pacific Ocean
Great white shark	All oceans except Arctic Ocean
Green turtle	All oceans except Arctic Ocean
Gray reef shark	Indian and Pacific oceans
Knifetooth sawfish	Indian and Pacific oceans
Sea otter	North Pacific Ocean

You can find out more about saving the world's wildlife by visiting the World Wildlife Fund (WWF) at http://www.panda.org.

Glossary

algae water plants with no stems or leaves, such as seaweed

ambush hunters animals who attack after waiting in a hiding place

barbs sharp points that stick out backward like a fish hook

camouflage something in an animal's appearance that helps it to blend into the background

carnivorous meat-eating

colonies groups of animals that live close together

crustacean a sea creature with a hard shell on the outside of its body, such as a crab

dorsal fin the large fin on the back of some fish

food chain the relationship between living things. It shows which animals eat which in order to survive

habitat an animal's natural living place

harpoons weapons like spears

lair the den or shelter of an animal

mammals animals whose young feed on their mother's milk

mollusks animals with no backbone, a soft body and a hard shell, such as snails

pods small herds or schools of animals

predators animals that hunt and kill other animals

prey animals that are caught and eaten by other animals

proboscis a special part of a creature's mouth that is shaped like a tube and is used for feeding

salivary glands body parts that produce liquid in the mouth. The liquid helps animals to swallow and digest food

scavenge to feed off dead animals

stalk to follow prey silently until ready to rush out and pounce

stingers animals that sting

tentacles bendable feelers that some animals, such as octopuses, use to feel things and to collect food

tidal zone an area where the daily rise and fall of the ocean, known as high and low tide, is extreme

venom poison that is injected by some animals to attack their enemies

venom sacs places in the animal's body that hold the poison or venom that they use to kill their prey

Index